New York Central
Power Along the
Volume #2 - Oscawana to Albany

Printed with pride in the U.S.A.

Photographs by Edward L. May

Commentary by Richard L. Stoving

The Railroad Press
PO Box 444
Hanover, PA 17331-0444

Copyright © 2005 by Richard Stoving and The Railroad Press. All rights reserved. No part of this book may be reproduced in part or whole, in any form or means whatsoever, including electronic media, without express written permission from the publisher, except for brief quotations used in reviews.

Printed in the United States of America.

International Standard Book Number 1-931477-17-5

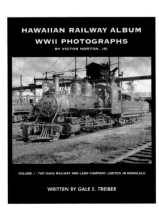

Publishers of:

TRP Magazine

PRR Lines West Pittsburgh to St. Louis 1960-1999

Illinois Central: North of the Ohio River

ALCO's to Allentown

Altoona Action

Passenger Cars of New England

INTRODUCTION

When a high school friend of mine popularly known as "Chooch" got his driver's license, he used his new mobility to go railfanning to places that had, up until then, remained inaccessible. On one of his earliest jaunts, he took three other guys along with him, one of them me and all of us a year younger, and headed for a location on the Erie mainline near Ho-Ho-Kus, New Jersey.

We positioned ourselves on the inside of a curve next to a rock cliff, got pictures of one train, and were promptly run off the property. We deserved it; it really was a terribly dangerous place to be.

So we decided to see if New York Central was any friendlier, crossed the Bear Mountain Bridge, and discovered the winding road that leads from Route 9D down to the two-track Central main at Manitou.

I didn't get any spectacular pictures with my Brownie Hawkeye camera, but Manitou itself made a lasting impression, and in the years that followed, I made many trips there. Of course, it was all dieselized by then, and you can imagine my thrill when I opened the pages of Al Staufer's 1961 classic, *Steam Power of the New York Central System, Vol. 1*, and found photographs of steam at Manitou in the 1930's and 1940's. The photographer was Edward L. May.

Eddie's first visit to Manitou appears to have been a two-day affair on Saturday and Sunday, July 1 and 2, 1939. He took 21 action shots there that weekend, three of which are in this book. The images are crisper than earlier action shots he had taken, because by 1939 he had acquired a camera with a faster shutter speed. Most of his earlier work consists of what he called "record shots" of locomotives standing in Harmon and other east-coast rail facilities.

Ed's primary photographic interest was in locomotives. He and other young men frequented engine terminals in the pre-war years to get and to trade rods-down shots of as many locomotives as possible, and because of this interest there are vastly more still shots in his collection than action photos. Of the 7,021 negatives in the core collection, only 584 are action shots; that's about a 12:1 ratio. When Ed did take action photos, the number of locations that he visited on New York Central's Hudson Division was limited. I once asked him why this was, and he said that it was more difficult in the 1930's and 1940's to take line-side photographs because of the many watchmen's cabins. Apparently he felt that he could wander with impunity around the ready tracks at Harmon, but that to venture past a watchman out on the main would not be a good thing to do. Eddie was not a pushy person.

A review of Ed's action photos suggests that he was more content to record the passage of as many trains as possible at a few choice locations than he was to find new locations and unusual angles. Although it is now often thought of as cliché, the three-quarter wedge shot was perfectly fine as far as Eddie was concerned, especially if there was an inside or an outside curve to add interest to the composition. I hope the abundance of wedge shots in this book will not be disappointing to the reader.

Ed made a number of his finest New York Central photographs available to Al Staufer for publication in *Later Power*, *Thoroughbreds*, and the aforementioned *Steam Power of the New York Central System, Vol. 1*. I chose to include fourteen of these previously-published images in this book, because it seemed right to me that a book of Eddie May's photographs ought to include some of his best work.

A word needs to be said about my use of directions. When I was a youngster, I asked my father to explain a sign that I saw at the New York Central passenger station in Dumont, New Jersey. It said, "SUBWAY TO WESTWARD TRAINS." My father explained the broader meaning of "subway," there having been at Dumont an underpass by which passengers could safely reach the platform opposite the station building. But it wasn't the use of the word "subway" that I questioned. "Why westward?" I asked. "The tracks are going north." My father was something of a railfan himself, and explained that it didn't matter which way the tracks were going by compass, it only mattered which way they were going by timetable. On the River Division, the old West Shore, the operating directions were east and west. I have invariably used these timetable directions in all of the commentary that I have written in this book. "Westbound extra," "westward platform," "westbound track," etc., all refer to movements away from New York City and toward Albany, regardless of compass direction at any specific location. You will not read of any trains going north or south in this book. On the other hand, in referring to something that is to one side of the line, as in "the building was on the east side of the tracks," and in referring to one of two parallel tunnel bores, as in "the train is emerging from the west bore of Oscawana tunnel," I have used the compass directions.

All of the pictures that appear in this book were personally printed by me. In most cases it took many attempts to get the best print possible from a negative. Some of the early negatives are too thin or too dense. I owe much to the memory of another dear departed friend, Hubert (Stocky) Stockwell, who taught me many darkroom tricks. Finding appropriate negatives, printing them, writing the commentary, and working to put this book together have all been parts of a labor of love, dedicated to the memory of the man whom I consider to be the Dean of the Hudson River School of Railroad Photography, Edward L. May.

Richard L. Stoving
November, 2004

ACKNOWLEDGEMENTS

To the best of my knowledge, there are only two photographs in this book that were not taken by Ed May. Both were printed from original but unattributed negatives in his collection. I am grateful to the person or persons who took these photographs.

I am also grateful to the several individuals who contributed in a variety of ways toward the completion of this book, including Richard J. Barrett, Abram Burnett, Fred Malan, Jack Shufelt, Charles M. Smith, Alvin F. Staufer, Paul Stoving, and Dennis R. Yachechak.

I also wish to thank Larry Auerbach, Maxine Jacobson, and Elaine Massena for the assistance they provided at the Westchester County Historical Society and the Westchester County Archives and Record Center. Further thanks go to Steven Gazzola, a researcher at the Putnam County Historical Society.

Thanks are also extended to Jaime F. M. Serensits at The Railroad Press for his support for this project and for his professional guidance.

Most of all, I thank my wife Nancy for her untiring readings and rereadings of the various drafts of the text, and for her careful reading of the final proofs.

Oscawana

The fact that the environs of Oscawana were in times long past frequented by Native Americans was not lost on at least one of Ed May's friends, who took many train photos at Oscawana and who, in writing for *The Railroad Enthusiast*, styled himself "The Oscawana Indian." The name of the location, which dates to the mid-1800's, derives from Askawanes, one of the signers of a 1682 deed to William Teller. A large portion of the area, including Oscawana Island, once known as Peggs Island, is now a county-owned park. Ed was a good speller, and he was always careful to avoid the common railfan error of spelling the station name with two "n"s, as in "Lackawanna." He was also mildly critical of writers who failed to observe the distinction.

ABOVE: The signal bridge about two miles west of Harmon provided an interesting background for trains rolling in both directions around the beautiful four-track main of the Hudson Division. Only about a mile east of the Oscawana station, it was an easy walk up along track 6, which can be seen just outside the bridge. This picture of J3a 5441 hustling #15, the *Ohio State Limited*, was taken on August 16, 1941, at a time when the semaphore-type fixed signals were being replaced with color-light signals.

OPPOSITE ABOVE: It's debatable which is better: an action photo taken from outside a curve or from inside. Certainly both have a lot going for them. This beautiful sweeping curve, also east of Oscawana, provided Eddie with a great location to capture the entire consist of any passenger train. S1b 6016 handles the 15 cars of #67, the *Commodore Vanderbilt*, seen here on April 7, 1946.

OPPOSITE BELOW: A day later, Eddie was back at Oscawana and took this photo looking west toward the station area, with the station footbridge in the background. The track on the left is track 6, an approach track for the West Croton yard. Freight trains carrying anything that triggered telltales at Garrison were routed to this track for inspection. The purpose of the telltales was to protect components of the electrification of the line that began at Croton-on-Hudson, principally the third rail. The power here is L3c 3064, built at Schenectady in April of 1942.

ABOVE: A recent snowfall didn't deter Ed from visiting Oscawana on February 23, 1946, where he recorded one-month-old S1b 6020 heading toward her rest at Harmon with an unidentified all-heavyweight train. Actually, the westernmost portion of Oscawana is an island, with a high rock outcropping that the railroad had to tunnel through. In this view from the eastbound Oscawana station platform, we can see the west bore of the twin tunnels that pierce the outcropping. The wooden crossing in the foreground was for the movement of baggage wagons. A fence between tracks 1 and 2 through the entire station area, with a locked gate, required passengers to use the footbridge to reach the eastbound platform from the station on the opposite side of the main.

OPPOSITE ABOVE: Probably just a short time later, DPA-1a 4007 and a companion B-unit rolled by with still another unidentified train. Ed almost always recorded train numbers on the glassine envelopes he used to protect his negatives, but this shot and that of the 6020 at Oscawana are not identified in that way.

OPPOSITE BELOW: Eddie was closer to Oscawana tunnel earlier on the same winter day to catch this mood shot of J1c Hudson 5253 storming out of the west bore with an extra east. All of Central's J1 and J3 Hudsons were built by Alco at Schenectady; this one was outshopped in December, 1928.

ABOVE: Looking east from the location at which he lensed Hudson 5253, and on the same day, Eddie caught streamlined J3a 5447 going all out with #51, the westbound *Empire State Express*. It's about 10 a.m. The 5447 has suffered many indignities since she was new and shiny eight years ago. She is filthy, some of her skirting has been cut away, she has traded her original tank for a huge pedestal-base tender, and her front coupler cover is missing. But she'll do her best to get 51 to Buffalo by the advertised 5 p.m., in spite of whatever snows may lie before her in the Mohawk Valley.

OPPOSITE ABOVE: A little more than a month later, on April 6, 1946, the snow was gone for another year. From nearly the same location between the eastward and westward tracks, Ed caught J1b 5204 about to enter Oscawana tunnel with #49, the *Advance Knickerbocker*. A timetable indication notes that this train will not carry baggage, and that appears to be the case, as the only head-end car is a milk car or express reefer.

OPPOSITE BELOW: The fireman and brakeman take a good look at Ed standing between the main tracks east of Oscawana tunnel as their 20-year-old L2a, the 2775, leads a 120-car extra west up the Hudson on track 1. This shot was taken on April 7, 1946.

ABOVE: Since there was considerable commuter traffic to and from Peekskill, it was common practice for many years to use steam power to tow MU coaches up the line for another 6-½ miles and back down. Engines laying over between longer runs were often used in this service, sometimes not even being turned at Peekskill. Here K11f Pacific 4594, fitted with footboards for its more usual local freight assignments, moves west with a string of seven MU coaches in a pre-war shot taken on February 23, 1939. This is an unattributed photo from Ed's collection.

BELOW: Lunging toward Oscawana tunnel under a plume of black smoke, S1b 6020 heads #15, the *Ohio State Limited*, on July 5, 1947. Four new stainless steel cars grace the front of the train. The bore through which tracks 1 and 3 passed was the first of several encountered as trains made their way up the Hudson, and I've been told that it was not uncommon for some local residents to gather up pieces of coal that were dislodged from the tops of highly piled tender loads here, to be taken home in baby carriages for domestic heating.

OPPOSITE ABOVE: Seen in another unattributed photo from Ed's collection, Niagara 6001, the first S1b, explodes out of the west end of the east bore of Oscawana tunnel with #63, the westbound *Water Level Limited*, on July 30, 1949. If truth be told, Ed did not care much for the Niagaras, calling them "just big power plants." They certainly were, and what most of us wouldn't give to see one running again! But beauty is in the eye of the beholder, and Ed's eye found more beauty in the lines of smaller, earlier steam power.

OPPOSITE BELOW: Just west of Oscawana tunnel, Ed caught DPA-1a 4005 and a companion B-unit about to enter the west bore with #24, the *Knickerbocker*, having crossed the curved causeway that the railroad built to connect the north end of Oscawana Island with the mainland. At this point, the railroad, going west, turned inland for about five miles to cut off a bend in the river. Note the guard rail on track 4. The hill beyond the tracks in the center of the picture will soon be the location of the Franklin D. Roosevelt VA Hospital. The date is April 7, 1946.

Volume 2 -- Oscawana to Albany

OPPOSITE ABOVE: Just west of Oscawana tunnel, Ed moved down to a lower location to catch #10, the eastbound *Mohawk*, about to enter the west bore behind 5-month-old S1b 6005. The hogger leans well out of the cab to get a good look at the photographer.

OPPOSITE BELOW: By the time the next train arrived, Ed had moved to a spot farther west on the line; the location can be seen beyond the rear of the train in the photo of the 4005. The two houses on the bluff east of the tracks also appear in the distance in that photo. This is J1e 5330 with #54.

CRUGERS

The hamlet, post office, and railroad station at Crugers, originally Cruger's, were named for the family of John Cruger, a merchant who arrived in New York City about 1700, became involved in municipal affairs, and served as New York's mayor from 1739 to 1744. His grandson, John Cruger III, established himself in Crugers, contracting in 1798 to build a large home overlooking the Hudson.

On a hill to the northwest of the railroad stands the Franklin D. Roosevelt VA Hospital, on land purchased by Westchester County in 1924 for use as a park but sold to the United States Government in 1945 for the facility. Metro-North has abandoned the stations at Oscawana, Crugers, and Montrose, replacing all with a single station called Cortlandt, now the only stop between Croton-Harmon and Peekskill.

ABOVE: Five cars of fresh produce for New Yorkers head the consist of this eastbound freight approaching Crugers in the care of an almost new Alco L3b, NYC 3031. The date is April 27, 1941, and the locomotive had been outshopped just three months before. She will soon be working hard to help win a war that is already raging in Europe.

OPPOSITE ABOVE: Where once she wheeled the *20th Century Limited*, K3q 4669 now has to be satisfied with #147, a four-car Poughkeepsie local. The train is seen here just west of Crugers, also on April 27, 1941.

OPPOSITE BELOW: Also west of Crugers, and having just passed under U.S. Route 9, (now 9A) J1b Hudson 5241 rolls eastward with a train that probably originated in Albany. The date is July 20, 1941, and by that time the fixed classification lamps on many of the Hudsons had been removed. They had originally been perched rather proudly at the front of the engines' smokeboxes. In my opinion, this removal dramatically altered the Hudsons' appearances, and not for the better.

ABOVE: The morning parade down the Hudson of the "Great Steel Fleet" was legendary, with over a dozen overnight trains mixing it up with a much greater number of commuter trains to deposit their passengers at Grand Central Terminal between 7 and 10 a.m. each weekday morning. The congestion was such that shortly before the war, Track 1, normally the westward express track, was signaled for eastward movements east of Garrison. To photograph the morning parade down the Hudson, a photographer had to be at trackside early, and Ed apparently arranged this on April 7, 1946, capturing the passage of twelve named trains at a spot between Crugers and Montrose where the low morning sun was at just the right angle. Let's watch five of the participants in the grand parade. Here, on track 1, comes the first section of #44, the *New York Special*, carrying sleepers off the Michigan Central from Detroit, Bay City, and Grand Rapids, with J1b 5244 on the point. It will arrive at G.C.T. at 7:20.

RIGHT: Next, galloping down track 2, comes J1d Hudson 5292 with #62, the *Montreal Limited*, bearing coaches and sleepers off Delaware and Hudson #8 and #10, and off Rutland #52, the *Mount Royal*. Note the two-tone D&H head-end car behind the tender. Cars from these trains were passed to the New York Central at Troy. Passengers will arrive at G.C.T. at 7:30.

BELOW: Back on reverse-signaled track 1, we have dual-service L4b Mohawk 3132 swinging by with #48, the *Detroiter*, the best overnight train from Detroit, carrying Pullman passengers only. This train will be due in G.C.T. at 7:50, on a precise Electric Division schedule that was measured in half-minute increments.

TOP: Now we see one of the "mighty ones," 5-month-old Niagara 6016, heading down track 4 with #20, the *Cleveland Limited*. This is another all-Pullman train with sleepers from Cleveland and Toronto. Notice that in almost all of these 1940's photographs, the locomotive headlights are not turned on. It was not until 1949 that New York Central changed operating rule 17 to require that a headlight "must be displayed on the leading end of every train and engine by day and by night."

ABOVE: As a matter of policy, New York Central generally assigned its newest power to its flagship train, the all-Pullman, extra-fare *20th Century Limited*, and in April of 1946, that meant EMD E-7 diesels. So the only train Ed photographed in the parade that fine morning that was not powered by steam was the eastbound *Century*, #26, headed by DPA-1a 4004. Passengers will arrive in New York precisely at 9:30. If not, management will want to know why.

ABOVE: Looking east from approximately the same location and on the very same morning, we have ample evidence that track 1 is now available for westward movements. Canting through the curve that will turn the line back toward the river's edge at Peekskill Bay, J1d 5296 leads #107, an early morning train that will run through to Syracuse. Train 107's first stop will be in Peekskill at 8:20.

PEEKSKILL AND CAMP SMITH

Peekskill, literally Peek's Creek, "kill" being the Dutch word for creek, owes its name to Jan Peeck, a tavern owner from New Amsterdam, who set up a trading post about two miles northeast of the river, on what is now Peekskill Hollow Brook, as early as 1654. He is said to have disappeared into the woods in the winter of 1660, but his wife continued to operate the trading post, and the area came to be known as Peekskill. The name later shifted to the area between Dickey Brook and Annsville Creek, presently the City of Peekskill.

The industrial revolution reached Peekskill early. In 1820 a local blacksmith turned his small shop into a crude foundry and began making plowshares for local farmers. It is said that after a while he was able to buy a horse to work the bellows, but that at first his wife had to undertake the task! His success was noted, and soon Peekskill had several thriving foundries. By 1880, Peekskill was one of the leading producers of cast iron stoves in the country, being the home of The People's Stove Works and the Union Stove Works.

Unskilled and semi-skilled workers swelled Peekskill's population to 15,245 by 1910.

Seeking a location for a camp and rifle range for the state militia, a military commission visited the area immediately to the north of the mouth of Annsville Creek in the spring of 1882. Favorably impressed by its proximity to West Point and by the availability of both water and rail transportation, they chose the site for the camp. No time was wasted in establishing the facility, which opened on July 1, 1882 with the arrival by steamboat of the 23rd Regiment from Brooklyn. Originally simply called the Camp of Instruction, it was named Camp Smith in 1926, in honor of the then governor, Alfred E. Smith.

Currently a training site of the New York National Guard, Camp Smith occupies 2,000 acres of property. It has been classified as a collective training area or an official annual training site for battalion-sized units, catering principally to light infantry, signal, and maintenance units.

BELOW: West of Peekskill, Central's Hudson Division narrowed down to two tracks, passing over a drawbridge and a causeway across the mouth of Annsville Creek to a location known as Roa Hook. At the time that Ed was taking his pictures, a curved spur trailing off track 1 and a covered platform constructed next to track 1 serviced nearby Camp Smith. Coming off the causeway and passing the platform, here is westbound #25, the *20th Century Limited*. Streamlined J3a 5453, seen here on August 1, 1941, appears almost as she was outshopped in 1938, the one visible concession to practicality being the absence of a piece of her skirting below the running board.

BOTTOM: Looking west from about the same location but twelve days earlier on July 20, Ed caught an extra eastbound freight behind almost-new L3a Mohawk 3010. The CCC&St.L boxcar on the right is spotted on the Camp Smith spur, and, yes, that is Ed's car in the picture.

ABOVE: Drifting around the same curve on the same July 1941 day, and seen from a point just a little farther to the west, we have J1b 5243 with #22, the *Lake Shore Limited*. This was the luxury train of choice before the advent of the *Century*. The footbridge over the tracks was one of many along the Hudson that provided people with access to the river's shore without danger to themselves on the tracks. It appears that Ed has moved his car and has been joined by another railfan.

OPPOSITE: Taken from the footbridge at Roa Hook, this photo of K3q 4683 with #147 shows the layout of the Camp Smith platform and spur. It was taken on Sunday, July 6, 1941. The train is carrying MU coaches that ran on their own to Harmon and are now being hauled to Poughkeepsie. The headlights on the coaches are a dead giveaway that these are MU cars.

ABOVE: A true Ed May classic and one that was first published on the cover of the April, 1942 issue of *The Railroad Enthusiast*, is this shot of J1d 5296 just entering the curve at Roa Hook with #41, the *Knickerbocker*. Train 41 made an afternoon departure from New York City and carried cars for Chicago and St. Louis. The date is July 20, 1941.

OPPOSITE: For some reason, Ed did not particularly favor overhead views; perhaps he just didn't like to climb rocks! Also on July 6, 1941, the footbridge at Roa Hook gave him a good vantage point for this view of J1e 5320 steaming east with #132. This was the *Henry Hudson*, an Albany-to-New York local-express that was scheduled to stop at Peekskill, about a mile and a quarter ahead, at 11:48 a.m. Eastern Standard Time. This would have been 12:48 p.m. by Ed's watch, because Daylight Saving Time was in effect. Railroads ran on Standard Time all year long, but had to adjust schedules twice each year so that trains would run when passengers, who had to live by whatever local time was in effect, needed them to run. If you were a commuter, and wanted a train to get you to the city about 30 minutes before you had to clock in at 9 a.m., you took a train that a summer timetable indicated would arrive at 7:30 a.m. On a winter timetable, the same train would be shown to arrive at 8:30 a.m. Confusing? You bet!

ABOVE: On Sunday, June 16, 1940, Ed caught L2c Mohawk 2875 blasting the skies with an extra eastbound freight and canting into the curve that leads to the final tangent before Fort Montgomery tunnel.

OPPOSITE ABOVE: On the same day and at the same location, K3g Pacific 4850 headed #148, a Sunday-only, late afternoon local from Poughkeepsie that made all the stops to Peekskill. The 4850 was constructed in September, 1913.

OPPOSITE BELOW: Eddie was at the same location on July 14, 1940 and recorded the passage of a number of trains with classic wedge shots similar to that of the 5215 featured on the front cover of this volume. Among these were four sections of the Democratic National Convention Special. This section, trailing one of the Pullman *Valley* observation cars that had been orphaned off the *20th Century Limited* by lightweight equipment in 1938, carried the Kings County (Brooklyn) delegation. The *Valley* cars were among a few of Ed's favorite things, and he swung around to capture this going-away view. One member of the delegation foregoes the schmoozing that was doubtlessly going on inside the train to enjoy the scenery from its rear platform.

Manitou

One who visits the area today would be hard-put to imagine the level of activity that once took place in Manitou. In 1863 and 1868 the Hudson River Copper Company obtained leases to properties on Manitou Mountain and Anthony's Nose for the purpose of mining copper. But because iron sulfide was found to be in greater abundance than copper, the Highland Chemical and Mining Company was organized in 1873 to built a plant to process the sulfurous ore on property in the vicinity of the railroad depot.

By 1877, it was reported that the company was employing some 80 men at the plant and 180 more at the mines, and that the plant was producing 52,000 pounds of sulfuric acid every 24 hours. Accordingly, the Manitou of more than a century ago boasted a post office, stores, a hotel and boarding houses, a school serving some 70 pupils, two churches, and, of course, several bars.

By 1886 the plant ceased to process local ores, turning to the use of sulfur imported from Italy. But high protective tariffs and improved processing methods made the Highland works increasingly obsolete. A 1908 analysis of the local ore yielded negative results, and in 1913 the plant was closed for good. The railroad withdrew its station agent in the following year.

A tiny Metro-North shelter bears the name of Manitou today, replacing an earlier miniscule New York Central shelter. A larger station, probably the same structure that was vacated by the agent in 1914, stood on the site into the 1940's and appears in some of Ed May's photos.

ABOVE: A little closer to Manitou station and also on July 14, 1940, Ed caught K3q 4669 with #156, a daily afternoon local from Poughkeepsie. The track in the foreground is a remnant of the nearly mile-long siding that was once adjacent to track 2 at this location, the only remaining portion at this time being east of the road crossing at Manitou. The spur served principally as a set-out track for cars found to be in bad order. The engine and tender are lettered in the new san-serif Gothic style that began to appear in the previous year.

OPPOSITE ABOVE: Laying down a thick plume of exhaust, L2a 2765 passes the same location a year earlier on July 1, 1939. The train is BRN-2. Ed didn't count cars this time, but a consist of at least 100 cars would be a safe bet.

OPPOSITE BELOW: In July of 1939, New York Central inaugurated the *Pacemaker*, an all-coach New York-Chicago service with morning arrivals, to counter the Pennsylvania Railroad's *Trailblazer*. To give the *Pacemaker* trains snappy-looking cars to carry the markers, two swallow-tailed observation cars were ordered, to be converted from open-platform observation cars 53 and 56 at the company's Beech Grove shops. However, these cars were not ready for service until September, 1940. Much to the delight of members of the railfan community, the company assigned two observation cars originally built for the *20th Century Limited*, *Catskill Valley* and *Seneca Valley*, to serve until 53 and 56 were ready. The ex-*Valley* cars were numbered 2598 and 2599, and painted in the two-tone gray scheme. Here is 2599 at the end of #3, the westbound *Pacemaker*, at Manitou on July 14, 1940. There's not much room available on *this* observation platform.

TOP: Her whistle screaming an approach upon the unprotected crossing at Manitou, streamlined J3a Hudson 5449 speeds west on July 2, 1939 with the third section of #67, the popular *Commodore Vanderbilt*. Behind her shrouded tank are reclining-seat deluxe coaches, a six double bedroom buffet-lounge car, an open-section sleeper serving as a parlor car, at least one diner, and a variety of sleeping cars bearing roomette, compartment, bedroom, and section accommodations.

ABOVE: Set well back from track 2, the position of the little Manitou depot betrays the one-time existence of the rest of the siding that once paralleled the main tracks here. L2c 2882 is bearing down on us with BRN-2 on Sunday, July 2, 1939, and Ed is enjoying an Independence Day weekend in the highlands of the Hudson.

BELOW: Hitting the same crossing at Manitou, J1d Hudson 5299 leads an eastbound extra on June 16, 1940. The two Pullmans cut in ahead of the head-end cars are probably being deadheaded. It could be a reflection, but it appears that this hogger has his headlight turned on.

BOTTOM: That there was once a long siding next to track 1 as well is evidenced by the set-back telegraph poles marching into the distance in this photograph looking west from Manitou. DPA-1a 4001 and a companion B-unit glide east with an unidentified train on May 6, 1950.

Cold Spring

The village of Cold Spring is said to have been named for a spring, located near the railroad station, that gave forth cold and clear water in abundance, and that for many years was used for watering steam locomotives. Cold Spring may also be remembered for the beauty of its location in the highlands of the Hudson, and as the one-time home of the famous West Point Foundry.

Cold Spring was a hamlet of only a few houses near the river at the opening of the 19th Century, but about 1817 a gun foundry was established in a flat and sandy area close to the Hudson River. As the West Point Foundry, it grew to be one of the largest general foundries in the country. At the outbreak of the Civil War, production was concentrated on the making of guns, projectiles, and gun carriages. Its best-known product was the Parrott gun, the invention of Robert Parker Parrott, the foundry's manager. Impressed with the capabilities of the weapon, President Abraham Lincoln visited Cold Spring in 1862 to inspect the foundry, and to observe practice rounds fired over the river at Storm King Mountain. Parrott guns were renowned for their smoothness of operation, range, and accuracy, and are said to have had a significant influence on the outcome of the War Between the States.

OPPOSITE ABOVE: Almost eclipsing milepost 51 on the four-track causeway just east of Cold Spring on the afternoon of March 23, 1941, New York Central's classic J1d 5295 speeds west with #41, the *Knickerbocker*. The first three digits of signal numbers 5101 and 5103, on the equally classic signal gantry, also betray the location, supposedly 51.0 miles from the north curb of West 42nd Street in New York City. Actually, the location was about three-quarters of a mile closer to West 42nd Street than the milepost and the signal numbers indicate, the distance between mileposts 10 and 11 having been reduced by 3,864 feet in 1906 with the construction of the Marble Hill Cutoff.

OPPOSITE BELOW: On the same causeway also on March 23, 1941, we see J1c 5260 showing a clean stack as she races eastward with #54, the *Mohawk*. While most rail photographers of the steam age welcomed the "burning-of-Rome" type of exhaust that lent character to their pictures, management had very much the opposite idea. Excessive black exhaust suggested wasted fuel and also infuriated the line-side public, especially on washdays in an age when most people hung their laundry out-of-doors to dry.

ABOVE: Having left Poughkeepsie about 20 minutes after the departure of #54 on the same day, K3q Pacific 4667 leads #156, a local that has somehow acquired two baggage-coach combination cars, one fore and one aft. The lead combine is probably being deadheaded. The K3q's were the last K3 engines to be built in quantity, 50 having been built by Alco's Brooks works in 1923 for New York Central, Michigan Central, and the Big Four. Five later K3r engines were built for the Big Four in 1925, but with somewhat modified specifications. The K3's traced their beginnings to the K3a engines of 1911, and their ancestry back to the earlier K2 Pacifics built between 1907 and 1910.

BREAKNECK RIDGE

No more challenging obstacle presented itself to the builders of the Hudson River Railroad than Breakneck Ridge, a Pre-Cambrian granite outcropping reaching right to the water's edge that could only be passed by the creation of an 842-foot, two-track tunnel, no easy accomplishment in the 1840's, using only hand-driven drills and black powder. Several contractors simply gave up on the job before one was found to complete the work following seventeen months of persistent effort.

Breakneck's rugged southern side, a landmark on the river sometimes called St. Anthony's Face, was quarried as early as 1848, when, with one terrific blast, an enormous block of granite weighing nearly 2,000 tons was detached. Quarrying continued until about 1900, supplying stone for a number of notable constructions including the High Bridge Aqueduct over the Harlem River, Brooklyn Bridge, and the base of the Statue of Liberty.

A second challenge met New York Central's engineers in the late 1920's, when the four-tracking of the Hudson Division was extended from Garrison to Beacon. Although more modern methods were available, it was necessary to drive the second, west bore through the same granite without interrupting the passage of trains through the east bore and without damaging the Catskill Aqueduct that passes beneath the railroad at this point or the adjacent shaft house of the aqueduct.

The vehicular tunnel through Breakneck Ridge was another late 1920's improvement. Before it was opened, the highway squeezed around the horn of the ridge next to the river, crossing the tracks at both ends of the railroad tunnels. The crossings were protected by watchmen and gates, but were still very dangerous because of the speed of trains exiting the tunnels and the limited visibility afforded to both motorists and enginemen.

Until 1933, the railroad maintained a depot called Storm King, named for the formidable mountain on the opposite side of the river. It was located immediately west of the tunnels. Metro-North currently accommodates hikers with a stop called Breakneck Ridge, a little farther to the west.

OPPOSITE: With a plume of white steam exhaust spouting from her auxiliary stack, one of Lima's L3b Mohawks, 3048, leads XN-2 out of the west bore of Breakneck tunnel west of Cold Spring on April 1, 1941. Twenty-five L3b's were constructed in 1940 and 1941, ten by Alco and fifteen by Lima. The Lima-built engines were easily identified by their semi-sunken Elesco feedwater heaters, the only New York Central engines to receive this rather unusual front-end treatment. The Alco L3b's were equipped with Worthington feedwater heaters.

ABOVE: Ed was trackside at Breakneck on June 21, 1947, and caught a mighty Niagara, S1b 6015, exploding from the east bore of the tunnel with #65, the *Advance Commodore Vanderbilt*.

BELOW: On an earlier visit to the same location, Ed photographed J3a 5441 roaring out of Breakneck tunnel with the first section of #67, the *Commodore Vanderbilt*. The landmark building on the right is a shaft house for the huge underground aqueduct that crosses beneath the Hudson at this point to bring Catskill Mountain water to the City of New York. The date is July 1, 1939.

ABOVE: North of Breakneck Ridge, the valley becomes broader, the river becomes wider, the railroad's tangents longer, and the degrees of curvature less severe. In 1938, the speed limit for westbound passenger, mail, and express trains went from 60 mph to 75 mph at New Hamburg. So it's likely that these two photographs, taken about three miles west of New Hamburg at Camelot on August 2, 1941, recorded J1b's "puttin' 'em down and pickin' 'em up" at something like 75 miles per hour. In the first view, Hudson 5215 is shown handling the second section of #163, the *Champlain*, while the second view shows sister Hudson 5204 knocking off the miles with #51, the venerable *Empire State Express*. The waters of the Hudson flow behind the station and section house.

Poughkeepsie

It has been said that the name of the river city that is located about halfway between New York and Albany has, over the years, been spelled in at least forty different ways. The present spelling is easy enough to master once it is remembered that the word "keep" spells the middle syllable. That the name derives from the language of Native Americans of the area there can be no doubt, but whether from *Apokeepsing*, possibly meaning "safe harbor," or from *Pooghkepesingh*, possibly meaning "where the water breaks," is a matter best left to the experts. What is important here is that the mid-Nineteenth Century construction of the Hudson River Railroad may be credited to some of Poughkeepsie's more forward-looking citizens.

Concerned about the economic welfare of their city because ice on the river caused an annual slump, and because of the anticipated completion of the inland New York and Harlem Railroad, certain Poughkeepsie businessmen made inquiries in 1841 as to the feasibility of constructing a railroad along the east shore of the Hudson. At first the idea was ridiculed, since it was thought that a railroad paralleling a navigable river would be absurd, but a charter was obtained in 1845 and the line was constructed in spite of much opposition from the New York and Harlem Railroad, steamboat operators, and many of the landowners along the river. The first train reached the Poughkeepsie depot on January 4, 1850.

The remaining portion of the line, from Poughkeepsie to Greenbush, was completed in 1851, and for many years Poughkeepsie served as a division point on the Hudson River Railroad, with trains changing engines there. Today it is the northern terminal for Metro-North trains on the Hudson line.

In the first half of the Twentieth Century, Poughkeepsie was probably most remembered for the boat races held on the river each June by the Intercollegiate Rowing Association. Teams from a dozen or more colleges competed, and Boat Race Day was as much a social event as it was a sporting event. Over on its River Division, on the west shore of the river, New York Central annually fielded an observation train that was essentially a rolling grandstand made up of more than fifty flat cars outfitted with river-facing seats. Cars reserved for the press and for officials were in the middle of the train and were kept abreast of the rowing crews during the race. Two locomotives were used, one on each end of the train, to effect rapid reversals.

ABOVE: Any New York Central steam aficionado will tell you that the last and most famous J1 to be built was J1e 5344. So if the Hudsons were numbered consecutively as built, what's with 5364? Well, this engine had been Michigan Central J1d 8219, built in December 1929, almost two years before the 5344. Under the 1936 renumbering, Michigan Central and Big Four locomotives were, in general, renumbered in line with the parent company's numbering system, sometimes resulting in older engines getting higher numbers. Ed said that he had just begun to figure out classes and numbers in 1936, when all of a sudden everything was changed. But he worked it all out in short order, we may be sure. Here's NYC 5364, no longer MC 8219, about to depart east from Poughkeepsie on July 17, 1937. A New Haven freight is trundling across the high bridge over the Hudson River in the background as the 5364's hogger looks anxiously for the highball.

BELOW: Probably the most ambitious locomotive rebuilding project ever undertaken by any railroad was the conversion of 462 class G5 Consolidations to H5 Mikados between 1912 and 1918. With the addition of 179 engines built new, there were more H5's on Central properties than any other class of road engine. Called "bulldogs" by some, the H5's were standard freight power before World War II on the River Division over on the west side of the Hudson River. However, few were seen on the Hudson Division by the time Ed was taking his pictures. But here at Poughkeepsie, also on July 17, 1937, is H5p 1375.

BOTTOM: Depicted in a photograph that is one of my favorites, #141, a daily New York-Albany train that made many but not all stops, heads west out of Poughkeepsie with J1d 5299 in the lead. It's June 24, 1939. One span of the high bridge of the New Haven freight line to Maybrook nicely frames the landmark spire of the Church of St. Peter, now the Church of Our Lady of Mt. Carmel.

BELOW: Camera in hand, Ed visited Rhinecliff, 15-½ miles up the river from Poughkeepsie, on Saturday, August 8, 1936, and he visited Kingston, on the opposite side of the river, on the same day. Whether he took the train or drove his car on this jaunt is unclear, but it's certain that he got from one location to the other by the Kingston-Rhinecliff ferry. Ed's collection contains five New York Central negatives exposed on that day, three in Kingston and two in Rhinecliff. Here's J1b 5219 at Rhinecliff with #160, an afternoon train that originated in Albany daily except Sunday. It would make all the stops all the way home.

OPPOSITE ABOVE: At Barrytown, the much-touted four-track, water-level main slimmed down to two tracks, and did not widen to four tracks again on the Hudson Division, making a lie out of the 1926 New York Central calendar depiction of the *20th Century Limited* speeding down a four-track main under the Alfred H. Smith Bridge west of Stuyvesant. Such is art. But it was a lot easier to maintain water-scooping track pans on two tracks than on four, and this was the case at Tivoli, about five miles up the line from Barrytown. Water scooping itself was an art on the New York Central, where locomotives equipped with tender overflow equipment could and did slake their thirsts over mile-long track pans at 80 miles per hour. Here's J3a Hudson 5441 hitting the Tivoli pans with the first section of #38, the *Missourian*, a train that Ed said invariably ran late. The date of this photograph, and the two that follow, is August 30, 1941.

OPPOSITE BELOW: A much lesser train, with two "twinkie" milk cars, two mail storage cars, and a rider coach for the conductor and flagman, hits the Tivoli pans at perhaps a somewhat more modest speed. This is J1e 5331 on an extra movement east. Regardless of the speed, a photographer in Ed's position had to be prepared to take a bath.

OPPOSITE ABOVE: As shadows lengthen, J3a 5437, hauling #67, the westbound *Commodore Vanderbilt,* takes a drink at Tivoli. The tall stack is for the pump house. The pans had to be filled quickly to be ready for the next movement. Double headers presented a problem; if the lead engine grabbed all the water, the second was in trouble.

OPPOSITE BELOW: A true mood piece is this going-away shot of the *20th Century Limited*, arguably Ed May's most famous photograph. It has been widely published, but any collection of his photos would not be complete without it. I'll let him tell the story, as he recounted it in Al Staufer's 1961 classic, *Steam Power of the New York Central System, Vol. 1*. "I was standing on the observation platform of New York City bound #2, the *Cayuga*. We were standing on a red block just outside Hudson, New York, when I realized the *Century* was due to pass. I got ready, hoping we would still be standing when she raced by us. We were." It's about 7 p.m. on June 28, 1936.

ABOVE: The farther we go up the Hudson the thinner Ed's collection of action photos becomes, and for several reasons. For one, the greater the distance he had to travel from his home on Long Island, the less time he had to take pictures. Add to this the fact that there was less traffic on the line the farther one got from Harmon, and the fact that the flatter topography and longer tangents were photographically less interesting, and you can understand why he catalogued 73 action shots at Manitou, but only this one at milepost 127, about twelve miles east of Albany. Super Hudson 5425 races east with #22, the *Lake Shore Limited*. It's August 31, 1941. The exhaust trail tells us that this baby is really moving; one wonders what Ed's shutter speed was for this crisp image. The burnished cylinder heads on the J3's lent a nice touch of class to these locomotives.

Rensselaer and Albany

By 1632, a settlement on the east bank of the Hudson River known as DeLaet's Burg was established at the mouth of Mill Creek. By 1655 it was known as *t Greyn Bos*, Dutch for pine (or green) woods. The area was incorporated as the Village of Greenbush in 1815.

By mid-century Greenbush had become a center of rail activity, with lines entering from Saratoga to the north, Boston to the east, and New York City to the south, and with the powerful presence of the New York Central across the river to the west. "Buildings of every description for the use of these railways are there in a cluster," wrote a commentator in 1866, "the most conspicuous of which is the immense, many-sided engine house of the Western Road, whose great dome, covered with bright tin, is a conspicuous object on a sunny day for scores of miles around."

In February of 1866 the first railroad bridge between Greenbush and Albany was completed, a single-track affair with a swing span that was levered around by four strong men to permit the passage of river traffic. It was jointly owned by Hudson River, Western (later Boston and Albany), and New York Central interests, and using it, Hudson River Railroad passenger trains were able to enter Albany.

As the Nineteenth Century drew to a close, it was felt that many of the old village boundaries had become less meaningful, and in 1897 a new municipality, the City of Rensselaer, was created, embracing the old village of Greenbush.

Situated at the head of deepwater navigation on the Hudson, Albany, the state capital, has from its very beginnings been a successful trading center. Its location was visited by Henry Hudson in 1609, and the Dutch built trading posts

ABOVE: We're at Rensselaer at last! Spewing forth surprisingly small clouds of "Alco dust" from its 2,000 horsepower, V-16 turbo-charged 4-cycle prime mover, DPA-2b 4203 gets underway from Rensselaer with eastbound #138, the *Upstate Special*, on August 21, 1949. One of Central's ubiquitous heavyweight baggage-coaches leads at least six stainless steel coaches, probably more. This was an all-coach Utica-to-New York morning train, with a diner-lounge car added to its consist at Albany.

OPPOSITE: Ed went on a two-day photography spree on July 1 and 2, 1950 that included visits to Rensselaer, West Albany, Selkirk, Colonie, and Schenectady, adding 86 New York Central and Delaware and Hudson photographs to his collection. He caught S1b Niagara 6010 bringing a mail and express train under the landmark overpass at Rensselaer on July 1, ready to speed east beside the Hudson to Harmon. Ed took a particular interest in New York Central, but his collection is by no means limited to that railroad. He photographed steam operations all over the east coast, with an emphasis on railroads operating out of New York City.

there in the following year. In 1614 a stockade fort was built on Castle Island, but it was soon swept away by a spring flood and fortifications were moved to the mainland. Fort Orange, furnished with eight cannon loaded with stones, was erected in 1623, and several families began a permanent settlement there the following year. By 1652 there were one hundred houses around the fort, and the settlement was declared a village and given the name Beverwyck because of the importance of the beaver in its economy. It was renamed Albany in honor of James, Duke of York and Albany, brother of King Charles II, when the English came into possession of New Netherland in 1664.

Albany quickly became a vital center for the transshipment of goods. It was the eastern terminus of the Erie Canal, completed in 1825, and in 1831 it became the eastern terminus of the fifteen-plus-mile Mohawk and Hudson Railroad, that embryonic fragment of the New York Central System. Rails bearing goods to and from all points of the compass soon converged at Albany.

Assisting in that convergence, of course, was the 1866 bridge across the Hudson, and passengers quickly became accustomed to the convenience that it provided. But a bitter struggle soon broke out between the Hudson River Railroad and the New York Central. Claiming that the Central had terminated interchange agreements, Cornelius Vanderbilt, by then in control of the Hudson River line, announced in January of 1867 that his company would only sell tickets and check baggage over its own road terminating in Greenbush, and would only recognize tickets sold at its own offices by its own agents. It being dead of winter, this quite literally left New York Central passengers heading for New York City out in the cold. The tactic so humbled Central management that Vanderbilt ultimately gained control of the New York Central. On November 1, 1869 a new company, the New York Central and Hudson River Railroad, was created, and Albany, no longer a terminal for two roads, became an important division point on one.

In 1900 the NYC&HR graced Albany with a beautiful new and spacious Union Station, which, as the corporate headquarters of a banking company, has survived urban renewal although the rails that it once served are now long gone. Close at hand is another survivor, the truly beautiful Flemish Gothic Delaware and Hudson Building, capped with a miniature *Half Moon* weathervane to remind all that its tower is said to stand over the very spot where the original *Half Moon* dropped anchor nearly 400 years ago.

TOP: H5p Mike 1595 makes a shove move on a string of tank cars at Rensselaer on May 4, 1946. The hefty 15,000 gallon, 18 ton tender suggests that this was one of the engines that had served as the primary freight haulers on the River Division between Selkirk and Weehawken before the war. Mohawks were allowed on this line only after bridge improvements permitted their operation.

ABOVE: Looking quite snappy at Rensselaer on March 22, 1936, this H6a Mikado, 5109, with a front-mounted bell and a deeply-sloped cab roof, has a decidedly un-New York Central appearance. That's because she was built to the standard light Mikado design developed by the United States Railroad Administration. The USRA took over the operation of America's railroads during World War I, returning them to their owners in terrible disrepair when the conflict was over. The USRA's locomotive design work on these Mikes, however, was superb, and dozens of railroads acquired them. New York Central lines got 194, all classed H6a. They were generally well liked by their crews, and five survived all the way to May, 1956. I have never seen a photo of one east of Rensselaer, however.

BELOW: Often seen on the River Division in commuter-train service, K11e 4560 was also hanging out at Rensselaer on July 2, 1950. I must confess a fondness for the K11's. I grew up in Dumont, New Jersey, where several of the class would lay over on weekends. In more innocent times, nobody much cared if a kid climbed aboard one on a Sunday afternoon and sat in the hogger's seat. Many fond memories remain.

BOTTOM: One of the engines that seemed to show up again and again in Hudson and River Division service is K3q Pacific 4669. In fact, photos of her appear on two earlier pages of this book. Here she is again, all coaled up and taking water at Rensselaer on September 29, 1951. She's a 1923 product of Alco's Brooks works.

BELOW: Here at Rensselaer on June 25, 1936 is the mother of Central's Hudson family, J1a 5200. Very much an experimental engine, she chuffed with considerable ballyhoo out of Alco at Schenectady on February 14, 1927 and soon underwent exhaustive testing. It's been said that the test crew fell so much in love with her that they made what they knew to be a futile bid to keep her for their own. Her performance lived up to the very best expectations, and 204 J1's in subclasses b, c, d, and e followed.

BOTTOM: Waiting at Rensselaer is B&A U2k 58, a Lima product of October, 1923. The date is July 1, 1950.

TOP: Boston and Albany acquired seven K3n Pacifics from parent company New York Central in 1937, 1938, and 1939. Among these was NYC 4741, which, under B&A ownership, became B&A 505. Here she is at Rensselaer on September 30, 1950. She alone went back to the New York Central in 1951, getting her old number back. This K3 is equipped with a Cole trailing truck, indicating that she does not have a booster engine. She doesn't have a mechanical stoker either. There was little rest for a fireman going over the Berkshires with this baby.

ABOVE: B&A J2b Hudson 608 was looking pretty much as built on June 28, 1936. In 1937 and 1938 the B&A Hudsons acquired big sandboxes in place of the modest protuberances with which they had been built, and as seen here. They were sand*boxes* indeed, big boxy things that did not do credit to the lines of these locomotives. But the motive power people knew what they were doing; it takes plenty of sand to get a heavy train over the Massachusetts hills. Ed caught this engine with her rods down, the pose preferred by the purists among the "engine picture kids." Some of these would even ask hostlers to move their charges slightly for the right effect, and quite surprisingly were often obliged.